Two Minutes to Shine

Book V

by

Pamela Sackett

SAMUEL FRENCH

FOUNDED 1830

NEW YORK HOLLYWOOD LONDON TORONTO

SAMUELFRENCH.COM

ISBN 978-0-573-66047-4   Printed in U.S.A.   #22320

IMPORTANT BILLING AND CREDIT REQUIREMENTS

AUTHOR'S NOTE

I thank you for considering and for making use of the *Two Minutes To Shine* monologue book series as you build resources for your auditions and artistic development! May your efforts bear fruit of all shapes, colors and textures.

Warm regards and gratitude to the delightful groups of actors who inspired appreciable portions of *Two Minutes To Shine Book V.*

For information about Pamela Sackett and her work as a writer and founding artist of Emotion Literacy Advocates™, peruse the following web sites:

www.samuelfrench.com
www.emolit.org
www.savingtheworldsolo.com
www.cdbaby.com

CONTENTS

MALE

SOON ENOUGH

idealist dodges delusion with denial

And so what if it does take that long? I mean, in the scheme of things? What if it does? At the rate we're going, we'll run out of operating capital well before then. Why push it? Whose measuring stick do you want to use anyway—yours or the bank's? We've got our own priorities to consider. That's *my* priority.

Look, we've been open for, what, 19 weeks? That's pretty good. We've served up a full compliment of my healthful concoctions to three to six people every night, most nights? So what if 99.9 percent of the world just don't get it? Does that mean we're wrong? Does that mean we quit? Every piece of mail we get, every phone call, every knock on the door would have us believing we should. What's quitting gonna do?

I believe in me, my culinary genius and my core philosophy and, ya know, if those places across the street want to keep selling their cheap, mundane, high-fat food to a standing room only crowd every single night of the week, let 'em. We're us, they're them; let's all be ourselves. And if those dessert shops want to continue taking people down the path of hardened arteries, pancreatic shock and triple bypasses, why compare? People will come around to the facts soon enough. We've got the healthiest, most creative product on the planet and we know it. Why hit people over their sick little heads with it?

Now are you going to call in your family tonight or should we just have mine over here again? Isn't this fun? You know, sometimes I think I prefer it this way but then I always was a sucker for challenge.

NOT FORMALLY

employee musters gumption to scale a height

No, sir, I didn't mean any disrespect by that, not at all. If that came across to you as disrespectful to you, I am sorry. I apologize. If you want to know *my* age...never mind, it doesn't matter.

Actually, I actually admire you. I have admired you for a long time. I work down the hall, way down that hall there in the billing department? And, I know you're from Louisiana* because your secretary and I have bumped into each other in the stock room and she knows I'm from Louisiana. I told her I'm from Louisiana.

Yes, no—no, no we have not *formally* met, no, but I just thought I'd introduce myself and ask you your age...crazy huh? I'm not the greatest conversationalist but I do try. Want to have some coffee some time and, uh, in the cafeteria, and talk about Louisiana and whatever else?

If you don't mind my saying so, sir, I think you and I have a few things in common—beyond the Louisiana connection, or we could. Your department is right up my alley, so to speak. The billing department's just temporary for me.

No, I don't mind closing the door, sir. I think that's a good idea actually. That hall gets awful drafty, sir. Yeah, right, I'll catch that door for ya right now. Yeah—yeah, yeah.

*adjust locale relative to accent of choice

PRIMARY NEED

brother offers love with residual motivation

It also refers to a female dog, wolf, fox or otter. So don't assume the meaning of my words. I could have meant a lot of things by that. In Black English, it just refers to a woman, in a non-derogatory sense. In other cultures, it means any number of things. One word can have a lot of meanings, it just depends on one's own meaning, one's interjecting, one's own interjection, injection. All right? All right!

You are a bitch! You are an unyielding, hard as nails, tough, callous, rude, rigid bitch! And regardless of what you think I mean by that...I'm an observer, I don't judge, I observe, I notice and I communicate. I share. Why bother having observations that you are not prepared to share and I'm prepared, for the first time in my life, to share my observations with you and my concern. I am concerned—you're my sister. I am concerned about your being a bitch—not judgmentally, not derogatorily but compassionately.

You've suffered the casualty of divorce because, and I'm observing here, people don't want to stay married to a bitch. Hal didn't—that's precisely why he left you. He observed, he reacted. Now what can we do about this? And don't tell me you don't need anybody because that's just negligent. You have needs too and they must be addressed. It's your duty and I'll help you. I am helping you.

Your primary need, and I'm observing this now, is to take your waning social skills in hand and convert them, as soon as you are able, into something a little more agreeable because you are your own worst enemy. Hal cared, he really did, but you just didn't see it. I'm not taking sides but the guy has a point.

Now if you're going to continue to be a bitch, my assessment of the situation is that it's not irrevocable but you're going to have to —

You're going to walk out while I'm sharing my observations? Bitch! Ungrateful bitch.

DROPPED

boyfriend covers breaking heart with well-kept focus

You dropped something. Did you hear what I said? You dropped something in the middle of my floor there and I would appreciate it if you'd please pick it up please. Hey! You dropped something else. That's two things you dropped now and I'd be grateful, I'd be so grateful if you'd pick those up. It's down on the—it just rolled under the chair.

I'd pick it up myself but I'm kind of tied up. I don't mind being tied up; it's not that. It's just if you're going to make a mess again, I'd like to get a little handle on that cuz, as you know, I keep my place in order.

I'm not going to try and stop you while you move your stuff out. I just want to keep my place in order. So can you ask your *associate* over here to untie me so I can keep my place in order during this mess-dropping exile of yours?

You dropped something…hey, it's spilling…don't spill on my rug. Can you wipe that up? Please.

Look, it's not going to be like last time. I have absolutely no interest in trying to stop you from leaving me. Believe me. It's just, you made a mess of my place last time and I'm trying to prevent that from happening again.

Hey, hey, hey—I never *gave* you that T-shirt. I lent it to you to sleep in not to wear outside—you've never worn that outside. Can you please fold that please before throwing it into the drawer? And can you tell your vulgarian if he has to pick his teeth, to do that over the sink please?

Don't be throwing my special pillow onto the floor—do you mind?!

Are you leaving me for good now? Are you going to come back in a month like last time? Is this the end now?

You dropped that….don't you want that picture of us? I gave it to you, it's yours, don't you want to take that with you? If you are *not* going to keep that, please pick it up, pick it up please. Look at that! It's going to get dog-eared.

FOREVER

older man reaches for last resort with desperate logic

Ahhh, what the hell—I'm just worrying and so are you—
worrying for no good reason. We're just a couple of
worrywarts—old married worrywarts. That's what we are.

Look through that window there. They've got white coats.
And look at these diplomas and certificates covering the
wall over here. These folks are real scientists. They know
exactly what they're doing or they wouldn't be charging so
much. You think they'd sell something this expensive if it
didn't work? Their reps are on the line.

Hey, listen to me…they promise forever and I die before
that—

    (snaps finger)

—they're out of business cuz I'll sue their sorry butts
quicker than my blood can fill their test tube. I die—as
predicted by that good-for-nothin' doctor of ours—they go
belly up. They *know* that so what are we worrying about?
I'm gonna live forever soon…as soon as they grant us the
official green light.

And I deserve forever. I mean that in an unselfish kind of
way. It's not like I'm having a great time and don't know
when enough is enough. My miserable life has been miserable—for *two* years! I deserve forever just to make up for
lost time and I'm willing to pay for it. I wouldn't call that
hoarding.

What's a second mortgage, high interest loan, stocks,
bonds, a couple of trucks and a college fund when it comes
to disproving that quack doctor of ours? They're selling
the one thing money can't buy and it's worth every penny.

RITE FOR THE JOB

young boy stakes claim with ulterior confidence

It's tough. I know. It's tough, but, hey, I can handle it. I can handle this kind of job. Oh I know you don't believe me. You think I'm ~~just a kid~~ ^too young^ ~~a thirteen-year-old kid~~. Hey, everyone's entitled to their opinion. But opinions aren't facts and the fact is I'm not a ~~thirteen-year-old kid~~ ^that young^ at all. I'm actually ^an old^ ~~a grown~~ man in a very young body. My body looks young, that's right, but inside I am big and I am huge and I am old—old enough for this job.

Your ad says you're looking for a male security guard and that's what I am. I am a big, huge, old male security guard. I like to guard stereo equipment because it's important. I mean if someone came into this place and jacked it, how would me and my friends listen to hip-hop? You do play hip-hop on this equipment don't ya? I mean if I'm gonna stand here and guard your stuff for eight hours, you gotta play hip-hop.

Here's my special technique: if somebody tries to take off with this stuff while hip-hop is playin', then hip-hop would stop playin' and that would make me real mad—swearin' mad—rude mad. I would yell—real loud. If I yell, that would stop your intruder dead in his tracks cuz when I yell, everything stops—ask my mom.

Do you want to hear me yell right now? I'll yell, right now, real loud and for a long time unless you give me this job, right now, for a long time. I mean if my mom can pay me to stop yellin' when she turns off my hip-hop, then you can pay me to start. So—when do you want me to start?

ALL THE BREAKS

young student pitches with multi-directional arm

So if you think I'm such a genius, why won't you go out with me? Just after my immense intellect, huh? Get yourself another lab partner, sweetheart, and good luck on next week's test without *my* shoulder to look over—I've had it with being used for my brain. I have a body too, ya know?

I thought you were interested. I really did. All the times I've asked you out and you never said "no." You never said "yes," but I thought you liked me so much you were playing hard to get. ~~I thought you thought I'd like you more with all those maybes but I couldn't like you any more~~.

I really thought you were interested. I loved thinking you were interested, however brilliantly false and ill-guided that thought was. But you know what? I love being your lab partner because you're fun and you like science even though you're not very good at it. And, I do appreciate your company; that's why I've asked you out so much.

I'll just go back to fighting off those sorority sisters next door to you over at Kappa Delta where my brains are of little interest because of their little brains. They just can't get enough of me over there. Those girls are relentless when it comes to staking a claim. My poor dumb body gets no rest. I can hardly keep up with them. They're just all over me—it's ridiculous.

It is ridiculous cuz they don't go out with me either—not so much as a glance do I get from them when I pick up my brother after he cleans the place. He's on work-study, my brother. I'm on scholarship. We smart ones get all the breaks.

BACK-UP

impeccable worrier animates trepidation with inanimate object

Are they still looking, are they still peering? You've got to get some proper drapes on those windows...that fabric, lovely lace, but they're paper thin—nosy ne'er do wells. I've never seen so many lights go on so fast. Of course, if *I* heard someone wailing like *I* just wailed—I was wailing wasn't I—I'd turn my lights on too. I just hope no one thinks we were fighting or like you were hitting me or something.

I don't know what got into me. We had such a great dinner and lovely chat last night about our future together...I'm sorry if I startled you awake at this late hour...some sort of horrible nightmare—horrible nightmare that was!

I lost my calculator—my old trusty calculator. I lost it... lost it forever! I was in the Amazon and the damn thing got caught in the Everglades. Those are in Florida though, aren't they? Odd.

I went looking for it with cardboard boots on—most uncharacteristic, unsightly things and highly porous. Then, you appeared, dressed up in some sort of sloppy jungle get-up, quite unnerving to look at and you were carrying my calculator in your teeth and there was a little drool, a little gray-green drool coming down on the left side of your mouth. I was sure the moisture—sticky unappetizing goop that it was—was going to seep into the keys of my calculator and cause it to commit an inaccuracy.

And then, nightmare of all nightmares, you swallowed my calculator—*whole!* I reached over, pressed into your navel, one time, with my right pinkie, of all digits. You smiled that same smile you smiled last night after you graciously invited me to move in here with you, permanently...and then your teeth turned into little mirrored numbers and I could see a full set of my own fragmented face flashing back at me. I looked wretched and worried and feared I'd never see my calculator again!

I'll just buy a new one, that's all, a little back-up, just in case, first thing in the morning. The world is full of calculators and nothing and nobody can prevent me from owning two.

AT MY DOOR

party boy shuns intrigue with open arms

And then she disappeared…it was 11:30, no, it was 12:30, maybe even 1:00 a.m. when I went upstairs to grab my coat off Kevin's bed, went back to the living room and found her gone. She just disappeared—until she sent me a letter two weeks later. And then she called me and then she showed up at my door. She never gave me *her* address *or* her phone number. She stayed for three days—and then she disappeared again…and then another letter with no return address again, another call, another visit—that time for a day, then poof!

Two months later, she rang the buzzer, three times—I just ignored it—then six times, then eight. She stayed for an hour. What do you think she wants from me? Heck if I know. Her letters were written in gibberish or they might as well have been and her phone calls were equally obscure—she breathed into the phone waiting for *me* to talk. I should have had her arrested for stalking.

I called Kevin and described her in detail but he couldn't place her, or so he says—claims he never invited anybody like that. I described everything—her hairstyle, clothes, car, her manner—all distinctive and excruciatingly gorgeous. I've asked around—no one seems to know who she is or how she came to be at that party.

I never should have talked to her or told her anything about myself. I told her everything about myself. I don't know why. I'm not the least bit interested—I don't even know her last name. Who cares? I don't—not at all—I'll make that perfectly clear next time. Do you think there's going to be a next time? I hope not. Do you think she's going to ring my buzzer—she better not. I know her ring—it's weird like she is. I won't answer it. I won't.

IN THIS LIGHT

man buffers anticipatory angst with ornithology and questionable promise

That was *not* an eagle. I know eagles and that was definitely not an eagle.

I'm not going to stay in this park all day, you know?

Not a mature eagle anyway. It was probably a raven. Immature eagles look like ravens, when they're immature. When eagles are mature, well, that's when they develop that majestic white plume of theirs—the kind you see on those postal trucks, you know?

Just tell me what you want and I'll tell you what I want to do about it. *Or*, tell me what you *don't* want this time. I can take it.

Probably just a raven though. Yep, just a raven.

Did you dress that way to torture me or are you off to an occasion?

Ravens can be beautiful in their own way, but they are not eagles. Now you'd never mistake an immature eagle for a falcon, say, a falcon or a hawk or a barn owl or a turkey vulture—all birds of prey but those ones are unmistakable. Don't look alike no matter what stage they're in—not at all. They all eat creatures—pluck them out or pick at them 'til there's no tomorrow, but they don't look alike.

I know you think I'm going to explode right here in broad daylight if you tell me you're not going to move back in for good yet. But I wouldn't explode if you told me that, trust me, I wouldn't explode...not at all!

You know, you are beginning to look like a bird to me in this light. In this light, you are definitely looking like some kind of bird.

EXPERIENCE

fugitive re-writes writing on the wall

Don't tell me that. We did not lose. Don't tell me that!
I know we didn't win. You don't have to tell me that.
I am clear about the whole package and that's what it
is—whole!

We didn't win, we didn't lose, we had an experience, a
whole experience, the likes of which I thought you had
before we met. You're acting like you never took anything
from anybody before.

Hey, would you close that door? Thanks—and lock it. I
gotta think. Shut up and let me think. Where did I put
those train tickets?! Don't count the piddly-ass money now,
just help me pack this shit up.

I'm not quitting. It's not quitting. That's just like the losin'
and winnin' game experience—a whole other kind of
experience—one I don't want to have. I'm having my own
kind of experience—it's called a moving experience. We
are going to move this experience to another experience.
Help me find those tickets before someone decides to have
a finger-pointing experience.

Does that rocking back and forth, does that help you? We
don't have time for that right now. What kind of experience do you think this is?!

IF I'M WRONG

dancer digs heels into shaky ground

Go ahead, jump in. Jump in! I do it all the time. It's easy. You put your feet together—like this—and then you tell them to get ready for the time of their life. *You* might be afraid but your feet aren't. Feet gotta dance, ya know?

Listen to that music—it's sensational. The band has it together. Sitting down to a beat like this is criminal. Hey, you're under arrest.

I'm not as scary as I look and, ya know, if you don't want to dance with me that's all right. If you don't want to talk to me, that's okay too, but, if you don't want to talk to me, then why the heck have you been staring at me for the last twenty minutes? You have been staring at me for a third of an hour, correct me if I'm wrong.

Are you *trying* to drive me crazy with those eyes, that hair and those shoulders or what?!

You see those women over there all lined up for a dance? They're waiting for the best—that's *me*. What are *you* waiting for?

FEMALE

OKAY

disappointed girlfriend builds case with stumbling blocks

So is this the kind of thing you think is okay to do to me? I'm just asking, is it? Because, if it is—I don't know.

Okay, so, you definitely do not want to go to this and you're telling me now, ten minutes before we're supposed to leave?! Okay.

This is really a screwed up thing, you know? You're a screwed up *thing*! I'm sorry, I didn't mean that. You're not a screwed up *thing*—you *do* screwed up things.

Is this your final word on this—you're not going? Okay, I'll go, and hook up with someone else. Okay? Okay, I didn't mean that—that's emotional blackmail and that's not okay. That is really not okay. That is *so* not okay. But it's also not okay for you to screw up our plans like this.

Don't you want to go? Why don't you want to go? Okay, you don't trust me. Is that it, cuz of what I did last time at one of these? Okay, I'm a flirt. So what if I am a flirt—I don't mean anything by it. Are you punishing me because I have social skills and you don't?! Okay, I didn't really mean that. There's nothing wrong with being *quiet*. But there is something terribly wrong with being totally quiet until the last minute.

I'll just go by myself because I'm dressed and I'm ready to go so I'm going to go. They say you don't have to be a couple to go to these and I'm not a couple, not tonight, so that's okay. Okay, don't worry, I'll go by myself and I'll stay by myself the whole night long because I wouldn't do that to you—even if the room fills all the way up with all kinds of really great and available men—because I just wouldn't do that to you cuz revenge is just not okay. Revenge is just really not okay. It is *so* not okay. Okay?

THE ULTIMATE TEST

boundary-crossing patient muddies waters

Last week? Yes, last week. Well, let's see. Last week, I finally told my boyfriend about you. I told him you asked me out. I know it was a lie but I had to see if he really cared about me and I don't think there's anything wrong with testing somebody. How else do you know when someone really cares? I could, flat out, ask him if he really loves me, but he could lie and what would *that* tell me?

Just when we started getting to the core of the matter in my therapy, some big urge for romantic reinforcement dredges up out of the blue and wrecks my personal progress. I think we were really getting somewhere too.

But then again, I think we're still getting somewhere because, otherwise, how else could I have been able to surmount my deep-seated fear of confronting my boyfriend about just how much he really does care about me?! I wish I didn't have to confront him like this, but you know my pattern—always attracted to withholding types.

I told him you'd, deeply and irrevocably, fallen in love with me. I thought that would be the ultimate test. If he really cared about me, he'd fight for me. And boy, did he ever come out of his shell.

It's really cool cuz he cried and he pleaded with me never to see you again. He begged me not to move out. I threatened that. It was just amazing how he responded to the prospect of losing me. He doesn't resent me, which is really incredible, but, I think he might resent you a little. How much I don't know but he did seem pretty pissed and ready to fight and who can blame him? I am worth some fight, don't you think?

Either way, I think we have a little bit of a situation starting up here. Do you have any professional suggestions on how we might proceed?

BIG CHANCE
revengeful sister exploits the art of relativity

I am dead serious. You go over there and tell him! Tell him anything you want. No, I'll tell you what to say. I don't know what you're going to say. No, I'll tell you, I don't know, it's not important, just get the point across. Scream if you have to. No, understate it, that's it. Do a casual, subtle, insidious kind of thing. No, blatant, be blatant. You're his wife—you can tell him any way you want!

You're too easy on him. He's a liar and a cheat. He deserves this. He's a megalomaniac. I'm sorry I ever fixed you up with him. And, he is ruining our relationship. I should have known but I felt sorry for him and wanted to help, so I gave him my best friend and now he wants to take you away—totally!

This is your big chance. I'll support you. Think about it—he's flippant with you, he under-prioritizes you, his birthday gifts are lousy, and he's a slob. Do you want to be married to *that* for the rest of your life?!

I say get out now before you're too old to attract so much as a parakeet. Or do you *want* to live in Toledo? Tell him to go try it out and then send for you. By that time, I'll have helped you state your case so stunningly, he'll be begging for mercy, give you three-quarters of his estate and it'll teach my brother the lesson he has always needed to learn—don't mess with your baby sister cuz your baby sister ain't no baby any more!

ONE GOOD TURN

lonely wife reaches for sympathy with iron fist

Don't look now but I saw that. I saw you do that. I won't tell anyone or anything, but, just so you know, you have been seen.

Of course I *could* tell someone I saw you do that and that would be a bit of bad situation for you, wouldn't it? I wouldn't want you to be in a bad situation but then you did something bad so that's a bad situation in itself—that would be two bad situations.

Why did you do that? Why did you take something that doesn't belong to you? That's just selling yourself short isn't it? Like saying this thing will never be given to me so I guess I'll just have to take it.

Gold medals must be earned, you know? And *he* earned all of those medals but I would have been happy to let you have the one you've been eyeing ever since my husband hired you to dust them.

He can do without one—such a busy man—one less medal to keep track of would do him good. And that would be *doing* good, on my part, to relieve him of at least one of his many preoccupations. One good turn renders another and could just cancel out something *some* may consider quite bad, don't you think?

I think—I think a lot.

BACK TO ME

high school alumni reunites misery with company

You heard me. We're equal. E-Q-U-A-L—the same. We are just exactly the same. Well, my hair's a little darker in the dark parts and yours is a little *lighter* in the light parts but other than that, our differences are negligible—at this point, this stage, currently. After all these years, our beauty is indistinguishable. Those bananas look a little too much on the green side. If I were you, I'd put them back and go for those yellower ones over there.

Used to be different, our looks, you know? Oh, what difference does it make? That was way back in seventh grade when you stole my boyfriend and I thought, "I'm prettier than her! What's *his* problem?!" But I didn't care, I didn't like him much anyway. Then he got glasses, dropped you and came back to me. And I thought: "Who wants him?!" Who wants a guy who wants a girl just cuz she's visibly better looking. Not me—that's who! How long are you going to be in town?

I heard Jeff's going to be at the reunion picnic. I couldn't care less, but, I heard he's got a paunch on him and I just want to see it for myself. My heart goes out to the guy, if the rumor's true, cuz he really had that appearance priority down to the bone and I doubt he's changed one whit. His belly may have, but not him.

I've changed—I have—haven't had a chocolate bar in eight years! And you?

THIS WAY

resigned wife turns corner

I am perfectly satisfied. Look at this face—is this the face of sheer and utter delight? Sheer and utter! No matter what you do! It doesn't matter if you flubbed this one, and you did, but, look at this face. Sheer and utter—amazing. And this time, I'm going stay this way.

I mean you can cuss and you can tell me to go away. You can insult me and embarrass me in front of our friends, like you just did not ten minutes ago. You can be ungracious to my mother for five hours straight and you can announce to the world that I am unworthy of your affections all my birthday week-end long.

I remain satisfied—untouched by your transgressions because I know who I am and I know *what* I am. I'm not up and I'm not down. I'm neutral—isn't that great? No more roller coasters, no more lightening bolts, no more hullabaloo. I'm forty now, grown up and acutely responsible and I can celebrate my birth without you. I can celebrate it that way for years to come!

I'm through with rage and tumult, unprovoked by provocation. I'm sworn to peace and quiescence—perfectly still, perfectly satisfied and about to be perfectly divorced!

UNTIDY CHOICE

pent-up defendant confesses skewed devotion

No, no, no, it's not that way, it's just, look, I told you my side of the story and I'm sticking with it. I mean it's true what I said. Everything I said is absolutely, iron-clad true. It may not make sense to *you* but it's true. I'm telling *you* my entire story's indelibly *true.* I'm telling *you* my entire story's indelibly *true.* Hey, that rhymes! So there you have it—rhyme and reason.

This woman that I love, that I love, like a sister…this woman that I've adored, that I've adored for years…this woman who chose to embrace her fears in lieu of my adoration— oblivious to it, for years! So I kissed her. No big deal—just trying to get her attention and what does she do? She hits me. So I hit her back a couple times, had to, no choice. Sometimes you've just got to give people a taste of their own poison. How was I to know she'd choke on it?

Hey—is it my fault the woman had a heart attack on the spot and dropped dead? I can't imagine anyone blaming me for *that!* I love her. She hit me. She hit me first. It was self-defense, plus too damn many cheeseburgers on *her* part. Blood pressure to the hilt since she was eighteen—I would have taken care of her…*if* she let me.

But no, she hit me instead and that was quite the untidy choice on her part. I could have had her arrested for hitting me first but she nipped *that* prospect in the bud. We could have been in here together sharing the sentence— and maybe even a few paragraphs.

(laughs)

So, do we have a case? We better have a case. I abhor prison food.

DRESSED FOR THIS
young mother-to-be births brood of metaphors

Of course I want to talk to you. I want to talk to you. Absolutely! I mean, you are the one I want to talk to. The question, the real question is, do you want to talk to me? And then the question after that would be, how much? How much do you want to talk to me? I've asked myself that question many times. This much or *this* much or… oh, what difference does it make? Since when does quantity influence quality, *real* quality and quality is crucial—the most important thing, I think.

That's the easy part. That's all the easy stuff. The hard part, the really difficult question is, how much would you want to talk to me after I tell you my secret? And I thought, well, I couldn't tell it to you here. When I was getting dressed for this I thought—not *there.* That would be highly improbable. You know, like bad math, *wrong* math. Secrets and family gatherings just don't add up very well. Don't get me wrong, I like these people, *your* people. I've liked them for seven months—almost for as many months as I've liked you and I have liked you. I still like you—lots. I've liked you lots ever since we met ten months ago.

I just never knew how *much* I liked you, how much my entire *body* liked you…and of course my mind and my spirit like you too—package deal! A full package…

(glides hands across impregnated belly)

…and getting fuller. I know you're still thinking about leaving, still. You said, right from the beginning, this was going to be an experiment between you and I—a temporary experiment. And I didn't fight you on that. But my body did. Go figure. I mean my body doesn't really want you to go. *I* get it, I get that you need to go—intellectually—but, not physically. I never was too good at adding things together. It's that bad math thing. I was bad at math.

Well, not all math. I was really good at subtraction. But I don't want to subtract anything right now…not you, not me, not anything.

EMPTY HOUSE

compromised mom compromises distinctions

I can just get up and walk right out of here right now! Don't believe me? Good, cuz I lied. I can't walk out of here right now and you know I can't. I can't go out of this house until you promise me one thing—that *you* won't go out of this house. Just one thing—you won't go out of this house after I go out of this house or I won't go out of this house and I want to go out of this house but I won't go unless you stay.

I trust you—every second of your glorious life—every minute, every day, I trust you. I trust you, my darling daughter, not the world, not the world, my darling a decade–plus–five years old. I don't trust the world.

Now we can't, the both of us, go out because if we do, someone is going to steal my liquor. So one of us has to stay here and make sure that no one steals my liquor. Last time I went out, my darling, you went out and when I got back, my liquor was gone and I just know someone out there in that vicious, stinking world wants more of it and if the both of us go out tonight, they're going to get it. And if they get my liquor, they'll want my food and my silverware and, before you know it, the house is empty. You wouldn't want to live in an empty house, would you?

Besides, someone has to look after your father and it's your turn.

NEED TO KNOW

anchor woman preempts public news with personal news

(crying)

Wait a minute, hold on a second would you?

(resumes crying)

Can you just…one more second.

(resumes crying)

I'm done. See? I'm done. Finished. It's over. I'm fine, really, fine, terrific, never been better.

(resumes crying then composes self)

What did you expect, I mean, you hand me this story and I mean it's awful, *really* awful. It is the worst story and it has to change. It's not up to me, I know, but somehow, what can I tell you, this story has to change. I don't like this kind of story—it gets to me and you shouldn't produce it. Do you want me to cry on camera? Then don't make me tell the world about this camping trip gone bad.

Why can't we do one of my stories or do I have to get past my probationary period first?! Ironically, I have this mother bear story. Listen, I just know it would increase our market share and be a real eye-opener—especially now. People need to know how hard it is for bear families. They already know about politics and crime, storms and stocks and million dollar deals for sell-out athletes of the week, but how about *real* people?! All right, bears aren't real people, but that's just because nobody understands them. Well, *I* understand them but that's because I grew up in a zoo. You didn't know that about me did you? Well, my mother worked there and that was her favorite cage to clean—the bear's cage. She worked that cage for years, heart of gold, and on her time off, which was minimal, what animal do you think she took me to see— now, *there's* a story for ya—Doctor Doolittle look out!

Now if you make me tell this other story, this awful story, people will think all bears are bad. It's not the bear's fault that guy left food out. Bears get hungry too, you know, and so do their children. The bear wouldn't have carried that man off if that man would have just let the food go. Let it go! But no!

FE/MALE

THAT ABSORBED

inquisitive person qualifies protracted premise

Forgive me, Father, for you have sinned. You have sinned! I mean *I* have sinned. I mean I have, I mean I was. I was told that. *You* have sinned, I was told. I was told that *I* have sinned. Someone said to me, someone said, to me, you have sinned. So forgive me, Father, for *you* as in *I* have sinned—have supposedly sinned.

So that's why I'm here—because of something someone said to me. Someone I care about...someone I used to care about. Is it a sin to have

(quotation gesture)

"stopped caring?!"

Is it a sin to separate yourself out for self-preservation? Is God against that? Is that a sin—to separate yourself from another *mortal* for self-preservation?

Do you separate yourself, Father? I wouldn't call you a sinner if you did. I wouldn't blame you one bit for trying to preserve yourself.

I know I am supposed to make sacrifices but does God really want me to give myself over *that* completely?

I know someone who would like that. I know someone who would have me do exactly that, ad infinitum. Only God is infinite though—right, Father?

That could just be something God wants to consider—to forgive someone for the sin of immersement, beyond all recognition. I don't look like myself when I get *that* absorbed. Is that what God wants?

And I got *that* absorbed. I think *that's* a sin. So forgive me, Father for I think, *I* think—for my *own* reasons—I definitely think I did, temporarily, for a short period, a few grueling weeks that ended four days ago...sin.

SOMETHING ELSE

gift-giver demands reception

You don't like it. You don't like it? You don't like it! I thought you'd like it. I was sure you'd like it. You really don't like it, do you? You don't like it at all. Oh-me-god, not at all!

How can you not like this? I can't believe you don't like it. It's perfect for you. It fits. It's your colors, it's your textures, and, you need it.

You've never had anything like this before—it's unique—different even...like me. You like me, so let's follow suit a little 'round here.

It looks good on you and it cost me a fortune. I took off work to find this. It took me months, that's right, and that was months ago—this thing has been hiding under our bed for months. If you'd clean up a little 'round here, maybe you'd have come across it and then you could have disliked it a lot sooner and we'd be done with this dark episode by now.

It's all right, doesn't matter. It's unreturnable. Got it from a street vendor. Well, he was a mime actually but he had some things for sale on the side and I thought, silly me, I just thought it was amazing—a hat/shawl/Frisbee/belt/fanny pack kind of one of a kind of thing like this?

I thought I knew you. I thought you appreciated me and what I had to offer. I'll offer you something else, that's all. You pick it out and I'll buy it. That won't work—I'm spent. That's cool, no problem. I'll sell the damn thing! I'll take to the streets and I'll sell it. I'll do mime if I have to! And then we'll go shopping.

AFTER THE OTHER

complaisant individual elbows edges with gentle jabs

They were chasing each other—fast! One right after the other. Chasing and running, chasing and running, relentless chasing, relentless running and then gone—both of them. I don't understand squirrels. Why they do that—that running and chasing and twitching? It's their true nature, I guess.

So, what's *your* true nature? Do you know your true nature? You don't have to say. Just think about it.

I think you're more like a bush than a squirrel. And that's good! You're a solid, stable type of individual—no twitching for you.

Still, I wouldn't mind a little twitching, a little swaying in the wind. I love the wind. I identify with that. I admire that—that gracefulness, that grace of a breeze—to move yourself with ease and, perhaps, even move another.

I'm going to move myself. I'm going to move this body.

We've been together, you and I, for one whole year and it's been wonderful, really. But I sense a breeze coming on.

You love this town and you apparently love my family and I love this breeze. Can you love this breeze, can you *feel* this breeze? If you can feel this breeze, you might just love it, mightn't you? You don't have to say. Just think about it.

FROM NOW ON

aspiring psychic unearths self from pigeon hole

That's right, my dearest darling, it's a game but a very real and serious game and the sky is your game board. And if you play your cards just right this evening, the stars will cast their brilliance upon you and you will gain passage to something new and something different!

But you have to believe, you have to trust and you have to remember: "if the sun and moon should doubt, they'd immediately go out!" Pretty good, huh? I'll bet you've never heard a psychic recite William Blake before.

Uh, um, now close your eyes, close your eyes and just imagine, for a change, you are in a dream—*your* dream—and in your dream, there is a road, close your eyes, a fork in the road, close your eyes please, close your eyes.

At the end of one part of the road is everything that you have ever wanted to know about your life and loved ones and at the other end of the road is something new and something different. Which side beckons you? Close your eyes...

> *(closes own eyes)*

...now take my hand and we shall embark down the road to dark space together and discover something new and something very, very special. Take my hand...

> *(squints open one eye to check on client...dismayed to see client head towards the door)*

....I said take my hand, not run for the door. All right, all right, I'll give you what I know you came for—the plain, simple, mundane truth...

> *(closes eyes to "see")*

...put your house on the market because it's going to sell in two days for three and a half times its original price. Your nephew's going to call you from Nebraska...again. And, oh yes, you are definitely going to get that raise you applied for with a better health plan, but not until Tuesday.

Well, there it is—you can bet on it—I've never failed in my predictions, but I'm sick to death of pandering.

Doesn't anyone hanker for poetry? Doesn't anyone crave the mystery in metaphor, the thrill of anticipation and a couple bars of Roy Orbison?—all of which I was fully prepared to give you with my mellifluous modulations.

Ehhhhhhhhh, don't bother yourself, Mrs. Conway, this one's on me, but from now on, I sell the sublime, only the sublime! Tell your nephew I said goodbye.

ELSEWISE

needful individual usurps own authority

A figment?! What are you saying?! It was a dream, nitwit, jerk! It was a dream! How much more real can you get... the dream in my head?! Now are you going to stand there and tell me I imagined my head? And what about my shoulders on which my head is placed and don't forget about my neck. I dare you to stand there and tell me I conjured *those*—those with which you have more than some familiarity. Touching is believing and you have believed all of the above, so, how about my dreams?

Believe me when I tell you, you crept into my dreams. You were the star. I thought we agreed to be casual friends. Well, according to my dream, you were some kind of all-powerful sort of creature and I was in awe of you. Look, it's not like I'm saying it's your fault or anything but I don't need to be in awe of anybody at the moment.

So, if you're having any inclinations, any thoughts, you know, to go the next level with me, you had just better think elsewise. And don't be telling me your thoughts have no say in the matter. Your thoughts matter, so don't be thinking them right now and you must be thinking them or I wouldn't be dreaming them. I have to figure my life out now and that's what I use my head for so don't be parking your thoughts in there.

Of course, you looked beautiful, as you do, and you were rescuing a small child from a terrible situation—a story to die for. Well, I won't be dying for anyone's story but my own, so just butt out of my head with your righteous self-concept.

It's my turn to be righteous and believe me when I'm righteous, I won't be rescuing a small child, I'll be rescuing an entire family, an entire community, the world maybe even! You find your own world to rescue, in your own head. Of course, you are welcome in my head on occasion but don't be thinking you're the man of my dreams, because I'm the man of my dreams. I am!

DELICATE DANCE

loyal extremist lowers boom

I just don't get you. For years you've been telling me and for years I've ignored you and you've chastised me every year, really put me through the ringer. But I put up with it, spend practically eleven months a year searching, because I care about you and want you to know it and because I just couldn't believe you wouldn't want me to get you *something* for your birthday.

So I do and you tell me I shouldn't have and you try to give it back and I plead with you to let me pamper you and you let me, begrudgingly, and I tell myself this is crazy, or I'm crazy, or don't know how to pick the right thing for you, but maybe you secretly like it and hate to admit it or maybe you really do hate my taste, but then you always seem to warm up to it, wear it or use it, show it off even. And I've always wondered if you do that out of pity for me and I worry, every year, that I'm putting you through something or ruining your birthday or forcing you to think about it when you wish you didn't have to. I worry it's my fault your birthdays make you just so unhappy every year.

So I thought I'd spare you, this year. I thought I'd take you at your word that you really don't want me to give you anything. I thought I'd go out on a limb and fulfill your long-standing wish. I thought for once I'd give up the great pleasure I get in letting you know, every year, how much I care for you and what you mean to me which is why, every year, I buy you something bigger, better, fancier, more expensive, more glamorous and breath-taking, more unusual and extravagant, but this year I thought I'd take a hint. After ten years of this delicate dance, I thought I'd sit this one out.

So what are you telling me? You like my presents, always have, you need them, you always will, can't live without them, not now, now ever? Is this little note you left on my doorstep your facetious way of saying thanks for nothing this year? You are welcome, very welcome indeed.

OTHER PEOPLE

cautious lover semanticizes perimeters

It's clear, absolutely clear, clear as a bell. Not to worry.
I get your drift. I get your meaning. Lots of people feel
that way. A whole lot of people feel that way. It's common.
Don't be afraid. *I'm* not afraid. I understand. I understand
perfectly.

So when was it you started loving me so much you could
die? Was it in Saskatchewan or Pittsburgh? Before the train
ride or after we caught a lift from that scary truck driver
or was it when we slept under the stars near that god-for-
saken campsite? I know, I know—it's when I danced for
you and tripped on your dog and ripped my shirt and your
dog threw up from too much popcorn and we laughed so
hard and felt ashamed and laughed some more and felt
ashamed—more and more ashamed.

I told you this trip would open you up. Now if we could
just turn the volume down, just a touch. I do want you to
love me but not quite so much. I don't want you to die.
Love does that to people. Sometimes some people love
other people so much they want to scream or cry or get all
extreme or something.

You don't love me that much, do you? I don't love *you* that
much. I don't love *anyone* so much I could die. Of course I
could die but I won't, I won't, I promise.

Do you promise? Then it would be okay. You could love
me as much as you want then.

SO FULL

dinner date hurls leftovers

Oh my god—what's *he/she* doing here? Don't look, don't look. Aww! Awwwww! Whatever!

Where were we? Oh yes, yes, yes—my definition of love— it's deep, fathoms deep. Just think of the ocean, the vast sea, miles deep, the Grand Canyon, but, but deeper. What I feel for you is really so much deeper.

Oh yuck—he's/she's with *her/him* now?! You've got to be kidding. Oh, his/her taste has truly disintegrated.

All right, I've lost my concentration, but I will get it back. You'd better believe I'll get it back. Don't look, don't look. I don't want them to see me...or you. It's just none of their business who I'm with now, none of their beeswax who I keep company with. They're probably spying on me. I wasn't the one who said I'd never come back here after we broke up—feigning torture and I believed him/her. This restaurant would just be too painful a reminder of our tragic ending, he/she said. No, no, no he/she called it our tragic pause. He/She needed time alone to think. Well, if that's what thinking looks like, he's/she's a brainless idiot.

So what is this love, this love I have for you? What is it? Well, whatever it is I'm glad I have it for *you* now instead of *him/her*. I love you so much I could jump for joy! I could skip and sing.

Do you mind if we forgo dessert? I'm feeling so full of love for you, I just don't think I could ingest another morsel.

Theatre artists share their experience:

"Pamela Sackett's monologues are a playground for an actor! With comedic twists and emotional turns, it's pure fun to sink your teeth into any one of them!"
—Freddy Molitch, actor, playwright

"There is no one better than Pamela Sackett writing custom-made monologues for actors. It is enervating as a director to have to sit through the same tired material day after day. Do yourself a favor, audition with something written by Pamela that is off the beaten track...you may get the job."
—Ted Sod, director, playwright, actor

"How can a two minute monologue reach inside your soul and shine a light on the deepest most inaccessible part you've been hoping to not expose? It probably can't—unless it's one Pamela Sackett has written for you. She has this uncanny way of seeing things you think are hidden and yet those very private things are just what's needed to make the monologue touch the souls of those who are listening to its delivery."
—Sue Ellen Katz, performing artist

"Pamela's monologues open a window for me to a character's world—the sights, sounds, emotions—the audience better hang on tight!"
—Michael J. Loggins, actor, director, accent/dialect/acting coach

"Pamela Sackett's creations are always incredibly fun, wonderfully interesting and just a little bit quirky which makes them perfect for auditioning! As a director in the theater, I rarely see actors truly joyful about their auditions and Pamela's monologues can enable them to be just that. The pieces in Two Minutes To Shine always have ingredients that I find compelling to see in auditions: character changes and actor choices. It is impossible to do a Pamela Sackett piece effectively without discovering those two delicious ingredients. Having worked with her pieces in my own auditions, with students preparing for their auditions and in workshops with actors for whom Pamela has designed monologues, I have great familiarity with how actors can joyfully play in their two minutes to shine."
—Molly Lyons Anderson, actor, director, teacher

"Pamela Sackett is a comedic treasure of a playwright. Her quirky and hilarious monologues (each individually wrapped and sized) make auditioning a joy!"
—Julie Daniels, actress, playwright, voice/dialect/acting coach

Other Popular
Monologue Books

by
Pamela Sackett

Two Minutes To Shine: Thirty Potent New
Monologues for the Auditioning Actor

Two Minutes To Shine Book II

Two Minutes To Shine Book III

Two Minutes To Shine Book IV: Contemporary
Monologues for Mixed Ages

Also by Pamela Sackett

Speak of the Ghost: In The Name of Emotion
Literacy
Saving The World Solo

Plays available from Samuel French, Inc.

THE OFFICE PLAYS
Two full length plays by Adam Bock

THE RECEPTIONIST
Comedy / 2m., 2f. Interior

At the start of a typical day in the Northeast Office, Beverly deals effortlessly with ringing phones and her colleague's romantic troubles. But the appearance of a charming rep from the Central Office disrupts the friendly routine. And as the true nature of the company's business becomes apparent, The Receptionist raises disquieting, provocative questions about the consequences of complicity with evil.

"...Mr. Bock's poisoned Post-it note of a play."
- New York Times

"Bock's intense initial focus on the routine goes to the heart of *The Receptionist's* pointed, painfully timely allegory... elliptical, provocative play..."
- Time Out New York

THE THUGS
Comedy / 2m, 6f / Interior

The Obie Award winning dark comedy about work, thunder and the mysterious things that are happening on the 9th floor of a big law firm. When a group of temps try to discover the secrets that lurk in the hidden crevices of their workplace, they realize they would rather believe in gossip and rumors than face dangerous realities.

"Bock starts you off giggling, but leaves you with a chill."
- Time Out New York

"... a delightfully paranoid little nightmare that is both more chillingly realistic and pointedly absurd than anything John Grisham ever dreamed up."
- New York Times

Plays available from Samuel French, Inc.

ELECTION DAY
Josh Tobiessen

Full Length / Comedy / 2m, 2f / Unit Set
It's Election Day, and Adam knows his over-zealous girlfriend will never forgive him if he fails to vote. But when his sex starved sister, an eco-terrorist, and a mayoral candidate willing to do anything for a vote all show up, Adam finds that making that quick trip to the polls might be harder than he thought. *Election Day* is a hilarious dark comedy about the price of political (and personal) campaigns.

"An outrageous comedy… at double-espresso speed."
- The New York Times

"Ridiculously entertaining… cute and cutting."
- Variety

"Laugh-out-loud."
- Backstage

"Delightfully farcical… Tobiessen takes a simple premise and spins it out into a hilarious sequence of events. His dialogue is lean and playful, and includes some terrific lines."
- Theatermania

SAMUEL FRENCH
OFF-OFF-BROADWAY
FESTIVAL PLAYS

TWENTY-SECOND SERIES

Brothers   This Is How It Is   Because I Wanted to Say Tremulous   The Last
Dance   For Tiger Lilies Out of Season   The Most Perfect Day

TWENTY-THIRD SERIES

The Way to Miami   Harriet Tubman Visits a Therapist   Meridan, Mississippi
Studio Portrait   It's Okay, Honey   Francis Brick Needs No Introduction

TWENTY-FOURTH SERIES

The Last Cigarette   Flight of Fancy   Physical Therapy   Nothing in the World Like It
The Price You Pay   Pearls Ophelia   A Significant Betrayal

TWENTY-FIFTH SERIES

Strawberry Fields   Sin Inch Adjustable   Evening Education   Hot Rot
A Pink Cadillac Nightmare   East of the Sun and West of the Moon

TWENTY-SIXTH SERIES

Tickets, Please!   Someplace Warm   The Test   A Closer Look
A Peace Replaced   Three Tables

TWENTY-SEVENTH SERIES

Born to Be Blue   The Parrot   Flights   A Doctor's Visit
Three Questions   The Devil's Parole

TWENTY-EIGHTH SERIES

Along for the Ride   A Low-Lying Fog   Blueberry Waltz   The Ferry
Leaving Tangier   Quick & Dirty (A Subway Fantasy)

TWENTY-NINTH SERIES

All in Little Pieces   The Casseroles of Far Rockaway   Feet of Clay
The King and the Condemned   My Wife's Coat   The Theodore Roosevelt Rotunda

THIRTIETH SERIES

Defacing Michael Jackson   The Ex   Kerry and Angie   Outside the Box
Picture Perfect   The Sweet Room

THIRTY-FIRST SERIES

Le Supermarché   Libretto   Play #3   Sick   Pischer   Relationtrip

THIRTY-SECOND SERIES

Opening   Circuit Breakers   Bright. Apple. Crush
The Roosevelt Cousins, Thoroughly Sauced   Every Man   The Good Book

SAMUELFRENCH.COM

Printed in the United States
215963BV00007B/1/P

9 780573 660474